Vitalize Your English Studies with Authentic Videos

INTEGRITY
Beginner

Osamu Takeuchi   Akihiko Sasaki

Daisuke Kawamitsu   Mizuki Moriyasu

Kinseido Publishing Co., Ltd.

3-21 Kanda Jimbo-cho, Chiyoda-ku,
Tokyo 101-0051, Japan

First published 2023 by Kinseido Publishing Co., Ltd.

Design   DAITECH co., ltd.

 音声ファイル無料ダウンロード

https://www.kinsei-do.co.jp/download/4174

この教科書で 🎧 DL 00 の表示がある箇所の音声は、上記 URL または QR コードにて
無料でダウンロードできます。自習用音声としてご活用ください。

▶ PC からのダウンロードをお勧めします。スマートフォンなどでダウンロードされる場合は、
　ダウンロード前に「**解凍アプリ**」を**インストール**してください。
▶ URL は、**検索ボックスではなくアドレスバー (URL 表示欄)** に入力してください。
▶ お使いのネットワーク環境によっては、ダウンロードできない場合があります。

⦿ **CD 00**　左記の表示がある箇所の音声は、教室用 CD (Class Audio CD) に収録されています。

Preface

In recent years, online videos have become an integral part of daily life for many university students. Within this context, it is becoming increasingly vital that such media be used in education to excite student interest in various global topics and events, as well as to further facilitate the development of comprehension and communication skills. The three books in this series aim to provide students with next-generation texts that utilize authentic videos to integrate and enhance the four skills of English, thereby honing students' skills in both organizing and transmitting information in English.

The *INTEGRITY* series consists of three books, organized according to proficiency level as measured by TOEIC® Test: the Beginner Level is designed for the TOEIC 300–400 range, the Intermediate Level for TOEIC 400–500, and the Advanced Level for TOEIC 500–600.

As this series utilizes videos to promote deeper learning, special emphasis was placed on the selection of the videos. Across the series, several common topics were covered, including social media, AI and modern life, environmental issues, human rights issues, urban issues, gender, and life and mental health, all of which are sure to stimulate the intellectual curiosity of university students.

In addition, the series adopts a "deep-dive" approach in which each topic is carefully examined in increasing depth and from multiple perspectives. This is achieved through four phases: "Motivating Students to Learn," "Comprehension & Deeper Understanding," "Internalization & Integration," and "Output." The series is designed to first spark interest in each topic and facilitate relatively effortless content comprehension. By having students experience various topics through English, the texts provide knowledge and simultaneously facilitate critical thinking, thus vitalizing students' learning and thinking processes through both tasks and the materials themselves. At the end of each unit, students are given an opportunity to express their thoughts and opinions on the topic in English.

The writing and editing team hopes that this series will equip students with the well-balanced command of English necessary to thrive in future society.

Finally, we would like to express our sincere appreciation to the editorial team at Kinseido for their efforts in making this series possible.

Early Winter 2022

Osamu Takeuchi (Series Supervisor)
Akihiko Sasaki
Daisuke Kawamitsu
Mizuki Moriyasu

• *Unit Structure*

Through the following four phases, students will be able to study a single topic from multiple perspectives and deepen their knowledge and understanding of that topic.

<hr>

PHASE 1   Motivating Students to Learn

1. Getting into the Topic

This section is designed to activate background knowledge surrounding the topic covered in the unit. It includes fill-in-the-blank and multiple-choice questions based on visual information. The information in this section is used to assist the video viewing in the subsequent section.

2. 1st Viewing

In this section, students view a video produced by *the Guardian*—one of the world's leading media outlets—and answer multiple-choice questions. The videos are edited to be approximately 1.5 to 2 minutes in length.

Note: the aim is to use both visual and auditory input to understand the main ideas and key information of the video, not to pick up every detail.

<hr>

PHASE 2   Comprehension & Deeper Understanding

1. Vocabulary

Students learn key vocabulary that appears in the subsequent Reading section in a matching task. Definitions are written in simple English.

The following dictionaries were referenced for the English definitions:

Oxford Learner's Dictionary / Cambridge Dictionary / Longman Dictionary of Contemporary English / Merriam-Webster Learner's Dictionary / Collins Online Dictionary

2. Reading

Students read a passage of approximately 250 words written in plain English. As the text includes background information and simplified explanations of the video clip viewed in Phase 1, students gain a deeper understanding of the topic.

3. Summary

Students read and fill in the blanks in a short summary of the reading passage aimed to allow students to confirm their understanding of the main points.

<table>
<tr><td>

PHASE 3

</td><td align="right">

Internalization & Integration

</td></tr>
</table>

2nd Viewing

The video from Phase 1 is shown again and students answer multiple-choice questions that require more detailed information. Students should try to make connections with what has been learned so far. Students are sure to notice that their understanding of the video is much deeper than in the 1st Viewing.

<table>
<tr><td>

PHASE 4

</td><td align="right">

Output

</td></tr>
</table>

Output Task

Once students are able to "own" their new knowledge, they can move on to output. After responding to personal questions related to the topic, students engage in tasks such as sharing their responses with a partner or drafting a presentation about the topic. In the final presentation step, the checklist provided should be used as a reference for how to present while keeping the listener in mind.

All videos have been produced by *the Guardian*.

The Guardian, which began as a weekly paper called *the Manchester Guardian* in 1821, is now one of the UK's most popular daily newspapers. It is most recognized for its investigative journalism and coverage of various social issues. In addition, its vast foreign correspondence allows it to provide stories not only domestically from the UK, but also from locations across the globe. The Guardian Media Group is like the Robin Hood of journalism, devoted to integrity and "giving a voice to the powerless and holding power to account."

Beginner
Contents

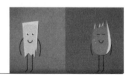

UNIT 1

Unique Travel Experiences

Do you like traveling abroad? If so, why? Is it because you like to eat ethnic food, or because you like to learn about other countries' cultures? There are a lot of ways you can enjoy traveling abroad.

PHASE 1

1 │ Getting into the Topic

Read the information about two unique, unusual places to stay in Asia and fill in the blanks with the appropriate words from below.

⊙ Hotel Gracery (Tokyo, Japan)

Stay in the special Godzilla-¹(   ) Room! A huge sculpture of Godzilla's hand on the wall makes you ²(   ) like he's just behind of you.

Sook Station (Bangkok,Thailand) ⊖

Want to experience ³(   ) in prison? Here, everything is prison-¹(   )—from the black-and-white clothes, to the ⁴(   ) on the window and the bunk bed!

feel	life	themed	bars

9

2 | ◼◀ 1st Viewing

online / video

Watch the video and choose the best answers to the following questions.

1. Who is this person?

  a. A criminal

  b. A journalist

  c. A prisoner

2. Where is this?

  a. A hostel

  b. A prison

  c. A restaurant

PHASE 2

1 | 📋 Vocabulary

Match the words with their definitions.

1. correspondent	☐	**a.** to make someone officially stay or live in one place
2. hostel	☐	**b.** a place where people, especially young people, can stay at low prices when they are traveling
3. outskirts	☐	**c.** the outer parts of a town or city
4. bunk bed	☐	**d.** a person who works for a newspaper, television station, etc., to report on a particular subject from another country
5. detain	☐	**e.** one of two beds connected together, one on top of the other

2 📖 Reading

Read the following passage.

 DL 02   CD 02

Experiencing Prison Life

When traveling, what kind of place do you want to stay at? A luxury hotel with an ocean view? A business hotel with all the latest equipment? These are definitely popular choices. Recently, however, more tourists have started to choose something more interesting and unusual.

5   Oliver Holmes, the Southeast Asia correspondent for *the Guardian*, reports about such a place in Thailand. "... This isn't a story about press freedom. I'm in a prison, but it's a prison you pay for," he says as he reports from Sook Station, which is a prison-themed hostel on the outskirts of Bangkok.

When guests check in to this unusual hostel, they are given a black-and-white
10   uniform instead of pajamas. "I'm gonna go [and] put these on. ... [They're] quite thick. It's thirty degrees outside in the tropical weather. But they'll do," Holmes reports. Every corner of this hostel has the prison theme. In the guest rooms, for example, there are steel bar sliding doors and bars on the windows just like a real prison. "[It] blacks out completely," Holmes says as he raised the blind on the window. There are
15   also bunk beds and pillows with covers in the black-and-white prison theme.

Of course, the hostel provides comforts such as air conditioning and Wi-Fi in the rooms as well. However, other than that, the entire hostel feels like a real prison. Holmes enjoys his unusual stay, but there is one thing he is a little worried about: he might wake up in the middle of the night and feel like he's really been detained. He
20   may yell, "Let me out!"   (268 words)

Notes

ℓ 5 *the Guardian*: a leading newspaper company in the UK
ℓ 6 **press freedom:** the right of the media to publish news or opinions without being controlled by the government
ℓ 8 **Bangkok:** the capital city of Thailand

3 | 📄 Summary

🎧 DL 03   💿 CD 03

Fill in the blanks and complete the summary of the reading.

Oliver Holmes, a correspondent for *the Guardian*, reports on his stay at "a prison

(**h** _____)" on the (**o** _____) of Bangkok. Like other regular

hostels, it provides (**b** _____) beds, pillows, and Wi-Fi. However, the

clothes provided are in the black-and-white prison theme, and steel bar sliding

doors and (**b** _____) on the windows make the guests feel like they

are really (**d** _____) in a prison.

PHASE 3

📹◀ 2nd Viewing

(online / video)

Watch the video again and choose the best answers to the following questions.

1. How much do you have to pay for this prison hostel?

   a. A lot of money
   b. Nothing
   c. Oliver doesn't mention the price.

2. How does Oliver like the thick prison clothes?

   a. It's very hot outside, so he doesn't want to wear the clothes.
   b. He thinks that the clothes will work although it's hot outside.
   c. He doesn't say anything about the clothes.

3. Oliver says, "I'm a little bit worried that I'm gonna wake up in the night." What is he worried will happen?

   a. The beds and pillows will not be very comfortable.
   b. The hostel will shut off the Wi-Fi.
   c. He will think he is in a real prison.

PHASE 4

💬✍ **Output Task** (Writing / Speaking)

Step I ▶ Answer the following questions.

a. Pretend you are the correspondent for a newspaper and want to report on a place for travelers to stay. What place would you recommend? What kind of place is it?

    e.g., I would recommend a Japanese *ryokan* in (*place*).

....
....

b. Explain why you would recommend that place.

    e.g., If you stay at a *ryokan*, you can experience real Japanese culture—you can wear a *yukata*, a casual *kimono*, and enjoy bathing in a spacious communal bath.

....
....
....

c. Add another appealing point about that place.

    e.g., Also, *ryokan* stays usually include delicious meals featuring seasonal local specialties.

....
....

Step 2 ▶ Put your answers from Step 1 a–c into a report on the place that you would recommend someone to stay.

a. Hello. I'm _____, the East Asia correspondent for *the Sakura Times*. I'm
　　　　　　　　(Your name)

here in Japan. I'm at _____ located in _____.
　　　　　　　　　　　　　a ryokan　　　　　　　　　　　　　Kyoto

I'm gonna tell you about it.

b. If you stay at _____, _____
　　　　　　　　　a ryokan　　　　　　　　　you can experience real Japanese culture—you can

_____.
wear a *yukata*, a casual *kimono*, and enjoy bathing in a spacious communal bath

c. Also, _____.
　　　　　　ryokan stays usually includes delicious meals featuring seasonal local specialties

So if you're planning a trip to Japan, be sure to check out _____!
　　　　　　　　　　　　　　　　　　　　　　　　　　　　Japanese *ryokan*

Step 3 ▶ Practice the report that you made in Step 2. Then, present the report to the class.

Checklist for the Presentation

Use this checklist to evaluate one of your classmate's presentations.

		Good				Bad
1.	The speaker speaks clearly.	5	4	3	2	1
2.	The speaker speaks in correct sentence forms.	5	4	3	2	1
3.	The speaker gives clear reasons for his/her recommendation.	5	4	3	2	1
4.	The speaker makes eye contact with the audience.	5	4	3	2	1

UNIT 2

Our Future Under Water?

The Earth is getting hotter and hotter because of global warming. A comedy theater group called UCB Comedy made an interesting video ad to bring attention to global warming. In the ad, some items are sold at very low prices and others at very high prices. Why?

PHASE 1

1 | Getting into the Topic

Fill in the blanks with the appropriate words below to complete the ad of an outdoor goods shop.

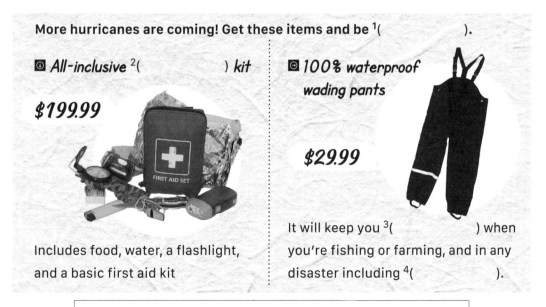

More hurricanes are coming! Get these items and be ¹( ).

◉ *All-inclusive* ²( ) *kit*

$199.99

Includes food, water, a flashlight, and a basic first aid kit

◉ *100% waterproof wading pants*

$29.99

It will keep you ³( ) when you're fishing or farming, and in any disaster including ⁴( ).

survival	hurricanes	dry	prepared

2 ◼◀ 1st Viewing

online video

Watch the video and choose the best answers to the following questions.

1. What is the year 2056 like?
   a. There is no summer.
   b. There is no winter.
   c. Everything is expensive.

2. Which of the following is sold at the lowest price?
   a. Snowboards
   b. River rafts
   c. Wading pants

PHASE 2

1 📋 Vocabulary

Match the words with their definitions.

1. **aware** ☐

2. **raft** ☐

3. **wade** ☐

4. **swallow** ☐

5. **expand** ☐

a. to become larger

b. to walk through deep water or liquid

c. having knowledge about something

d. to make food, drink, etc. go down your throat

e. a flat boat for traveling through water

2 📖 Reading

Read the following passage.

Climate Change Bargains 2056

Human activity has caused the planet to heat up. As it gets hotter, the Earth becomes a more difficult place to live in. The first step to solving the global warming problem is to make people more aware of it. UCB Comedy, a comedy theater group from the US, uses humor to raise awareness about global warming. They made a
5　video ad set in the year 2056 for an imaginary department store, "Stuff Mart."

On the one hand, items people no longer need in 2056 are on sale. In a world with no winter, who needs heavy coats or warm scarves? Stuff Mart cannot sell these items anymore, so you can buy two coats or three scarves for the price of one. Snowboards are "just boards" in a world with no snow, so you can get as many snowboards as you
10　like for just $5.

On the other hand, some items are much more expensive. Global warming has caused water levels to rise, so Stuff Mart is selling river rafts for $45,000. In addition, everyone will need wading pants to walk outside, so they cost $900. Stuff Mart recommends everyone should buy a survival kit because now every season is
15　hurricane season. If you spend over $500 at the store, you also receive a free ice cube. It will remind you what cold felt like.

Would you like to visit Stuff Mart? If so, you had better go before we are all swallowed by the expanding sea! If the sea level continues to rise, even Stuff Mart will be under water.　　　　　　　　　　　　　　　　　　　(261 words)

Note

ℓ 3　**UCB Comedy:** a theater group that teaches and creates comedy; run by the Upright Citizens Brigade Theater, which was founded in 1999 and is famous for its improv (acting without scripts)

3 | 📄 Summary

🎧 DL 05   ⏺ CD 05

Fill in the blanks and complete the summary of the reading.

UCB Comedy made a video ad to raise (**a**   ) about global warming. In the ad set in 2056, coats, (**s**   ), and snowboards are very cheap because there is no more (**w**   ). However, river rafts, (**w**   ) pants, and (**s**   ) kits are now very expensive because there are a lot of hurricanes in 2056.

PHASE 3

◼️◀ 2nd Viewing

online / video

Watch the video again and choose the best answers to the following questions.

1. The female narrator says, "what better place to take shelter from skin-melting temperatures than Stuff Mart?" What does "skin-melting temperatures" mean?

   a. Very high temperatures
   b. Normal temperatures
   c. Very low temperatures

2. Which of the following sets of survival kits is the most expensive?

   a. 3-day kits × 10
   b. 5-day kits × 6
   c. 30-day kit × 1

3. At the end of the ad, the female narrator says, "Come on into Stuff Mart today." Why?

   a. Because Stuff Mart is not very busy today
   b. Because Stuff Mart may be under water soon
   c. Because Stuff Mart is closed tomorrow

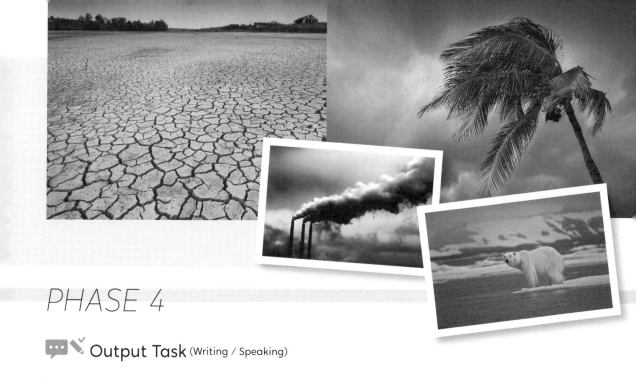

PHASE 4

💬✔ **Output Task** (Writing / Speaking)

Step 1 ▶ Answer the following questions.

a. What kind of stuff would become unnecessary if global warming made winter disappear?

e.g., I think that "kotatsu" would become unnecessary.

b. What kind of activities would you be unable to do if global warming made winter disappear?

e.g., We would be unable to go skiing.

c. How would you feel if there were hot summers all year round? Why?

e.g., I would feel very sad because I like winter the best of all seasons.

Step 2 Ask a partner the questions from the previous page and complete the sentences below.

a. If global warming made winter disappear, my partner, _____,
(your partner's name)

thshinks that _____ would become unnecessary.
heaters

b. He/She also says that we would be unable to _____.
have snowball fights

c. If there were hot summers all year round, he/she would feel _____
very irritated

_____ because he/she _____
doesn't like hot weather

_____.

Step 3 Practice the report that you made in Step 2. Then, present the report to the class.

Checklist for the Presentation

Use this checklist to evaluate one of your classmate's presentations.

		Good				Bad
1.	The speaker speaks clearly.	5	4	3	2	1
2.	The speaker speaks in correct sentence forms.	5	4	3	2	1
3.	The speaker gives clear reasons for his/her partner's statement.	5	4	3	2	1
4.	The speaker makes eye contact with the audience.	5	4	3	2	1

UNIT 3

A DIY-Sushi Party with Friends

Have you ever made sushi? Do you know how to make it? Makiko Sano explains how to make sushi and invites her friends to a DIY-sushi party. She really likes to serve sushi to her friends at home.

PHASE 1

1 | Getting into the Topic

Read about two different types of sushi and fill in the blanks with the appropriate words from below.

Around the eighth century

Narezushi

This is the earliest form of sushi. By pickling rice and fish together, people made it last for a long time. Even ¹( ) took it with them!

Present

Nigirizushi

Nigirizushi is hand-formed vinegared rice topped with a main ²( ). The most common ingredient is ³( ) fish, such as salmon, tuna, or ⁴( ).

ingredient	raw	travelers	yellowtail

21

2 📹 1st Viewing

online video

Watch the video and choose the best answers to the following questions.

1. What is Makiko NOT doing?

    a. Eating sushi at a restaurant

    b. Making sushi

    c. Talking about how to make sushi

2. What fish does Makiko like?

    a. Salmon

    b. Yellowtail

    c. Tuna

PHASE 2

1 📋 Vocabulary

Match the words with their definitions.

1. serve

    a. difficult to hold because of being smooth, wet, or oily

2. ingredients

    b. things used to make a particular dish

3. edge

    c. to give people food and drink

4. slippery

    d. the sharp or narrow side of something

5. treat

    e. to arrange something special for someone

2 📖 Reading

Read the following passage.

 DL 06   CD 06

How to Make Sushi with Friends

A Japanese woman, Makiko Sano, lives in the UK. She often serves sushi at celebrations. She likes to choose raw fish ingredients for each event and guest, and hold a sushi party at home. She calls it DIY-sushi. She likes to meet with her friends and family. It's especially fun for her to hold sushi parties because she loves not only

5 to see people enjoying the sushi she has made, but also to talk with them about their favorite sushi.

Many people think that it's very hard to make sushi, but Makiko says it's not difficult at all. According to her, there are some tricks to making good DIY-sushi at home. First of all, it's important that the knife is sharp when cutting the fish. Second,

10 the cook should have a wet towel to wipe the edge of the knife with because the fish oil makes the knife very slippery. Third, the fish needs to be sliced thinly, but it doesn't have to be as thin as smoked salmon.

When she came to the UK for the first time, Makiko found that sushi was quite an unusual dish for Western people because they were not used to touching rice with

15 their bare hands to make it. However, more and more people have gotten used to it and enjoy making and eating sushi at parties. For Makiko, serving sushi at home is a way to treat her friends to a little bit of a special meal.   (245 words)

Notes

ℓ 3 **DIY:** the activity of making or repairing things yourself; an abbreviation of "do-it-yourself"

3 📄 Summary

🎧 DL 07   💿 CD 07

Fill in the blanks and complete the summary of the reading.

Makiko Sano often serves sushi for (**c**   ). She loves to see people enjoying the sushi that she has made. She also loves to see people (**t**   ) about their favorite sushi. According to her, there are some (**t**   ) to making good DIY-sushi. One of them is that the knife needs to be (**s**   ). She says that serving sushi at home is a way to treat her friends to a little bit of a (**s**   ) meal.

PHASE 3

◼◀ 2nd Viewing

online video

Watch the video again and choose the best answers to the following questions.

1. According to Makiko, what do the kanji characters for sushi mean?

   a. Celebration
   b. Tokyo
   c. Travelers

2. Why do you need to slice the fish thin when you make sushi?

   a. Because everyone likes smoked salmon
   b. Because a chunk of fish is very hard to chew
   c. Makiko doesn't mention the answer.

3. Who is NOT attending the DIY-sushi party?

   a. Makiko's Japanese friends
   b. Businessmen
   c. A university teacher

PHASE 4

💬✍ Output Task (Writing / Speaking)

 **Step 1** Answer the following questions.

a. If you had a home party at your house, what would you serve to your friends?

e.g., I would serve curry and rice to my friends.

....

....

b. Why? Explain your reasons.

e.g., Because I am good at making curry and I can put my friends' favorite ingredients in it.

....

....

....

Step 2 Ask a partner the questions from the previous page and complete the sentences below.

a. My partner, _____ , will _____
(your partner's name)   *serve okonomiyaki to his/her friends*

_____

b. because _____
okonomiyaki is healthy and has many variations

_____ .

Step 3 Practice the report that you made in Step 2. Then, present the report to the class.

Checklist for the Presentation

Use this checklist to evaluate one of your classmate's presentations.

		Good				Bad
1.	The speaker speaks clearly.	5	4	3	2	1
2.	The speaker speaks in correct sentence forms.	5	4	3	2	1
3.	The speaker gives clear reasons for his/her partner's statement.	5	4	3	2	1
4.	The speaker makes eye contact with the audience.	5	4	3	2	1

UNIT 4

Naughty but Lovely: Australia's Cockatoos

There are a lot of attractive birds in Australia. Sulphur-crested cockatoos are one kind of interesting bird and are known as one of the funniest and friendliest birds. Some people keep them as pets, but sulphur-crested cockatoos in Katoomba sometimes cause trouble for the people of the town.

PHASE 1

1 Getting into the Topic

Read the following quick facts about sulphur-crested cockatoos and fill in the blanks with the appropriate words from below.

Sulphur-crested cockatoos: Quick Facts

Habitat: Northern and eastern [1](   ), New Guinea, Indonesia and Palau

In Australia, these cockatoos are found mostly in open forests and [2](   ).

Characteristics: Naughty, affectionate, and [3](   )

You Should Know: They learn quickly by mimicking and can teach each other how to open the lid of a [4](   ) can.

| farmlands | intelligent | Australia | garbage |

27

2 | ◉◀ 1st Viewing

Watch the video and choose the best answers to the following questions.

1. How do the cockatoos in the video look?
   a. Calm
   b. Gentle
   c. Naughty

2. How do people in the town seem to feel about the cockatoos?
   a. They don't care.
   b. They hate them.
   c. They love them.

PHASE 2

1 | 📋 Vocabulary

Match the words with their definitions.

1. **naughty**

2. **scatter**

3. **notorious**

4. **enthusiast**

5. **weed**

a. a person who is very interested in a particular topic or activity

b. a wild plant growing in an unwanted place

c. badly behaved

d. famous for something bad

e. to throw or drop something over a large area in an irregular way

Read the following passage. DL 08 CD 08

Watching Australia's Naughtiest Cockatoo

Sulphur-crested cockatoos are one of Australia's smartest and naughtiest birds. They are known to bully other animals, such as small birds and cats, open the lids of garbage cans on the street, and scatter garbage to look for food. They are also notorious for destroying wooden balconies, roofs, and the window frames of houses.
5 They cut off the tops of flowers, pull out small plants, pick at trees, and generally make a big mess.

Stephanie Convery, a journalist and cockatoo enthusiast, visited the town of Katoomba in the Blue Mountains, which is called the home of the sulphur-crested cockatoo. People in the town told Stephanie that they were annoyed with the
10 cockatoos' naughty behaviors. For example, the cockatoos were taking the bird spikes off of the buildings and pulling out the rubber lining from between the doors and the roofs of the cars. People also said that there were more cockatoos than five years before. Now, a lot of cockatoos are found along Katoomba Street. These cockatoos are friendly to tourists. Some people in Katoomba worry about the cockatoos getting fat
15 because the tourists like to feed them!

One woman said that cockatoos have become "weeds," which means they are not wanted in certain areas because their numbers have become so large. Indeed, cockatoos are sometimes a nuisance—they drop their feathers everywhere and screech loudly every morning—but the people of Katoomba do not hate them. People still love them for their funny and humorous characters.   (247 words)

Notes

ℓ 8 **Katoomba in the Blue Mountains:** the chief town of the City of Blue Mountains in New South Wales, Australia, located about 100 km west of Sydney

ℓ 10 **bird spikes:** thin, sharp pointed pieces of metal put on walls or railings to stop birds from coming to rest

ℓ 11 **rubber lining:** a layer of rubber material that covers the inside surface of something

3 📄 Summary 🎧 DL 09 💿 CD 09

Fill in the blanks and complete the summary of the reading.

Sulphur-crested cockatoos are known as one of the (**n**   ) birds in Australia. In Katoomba, where a lot of the cockatoos live, their (**n**   ) have become very large and people are getting (**a**   ) with their bad behavior. Indeed, these cockatoos are sometimes a (**n**   ), but the people of Katoomba still love the cockatoos' funny and humorous (**c**   ).

PHASE 3

🎥 2nd Viewing   online/video

Watch the video again and choose the best answers to the following questions.

1. What did Melanie Weine mean by "A number of them now are regular visitors to the bakery?"

   a. Many people now visit the bakery regularly.
   b. Regular visitors to the bakery are increasing now.
   c. Many cockatoos are now often sitting at the bakery.

2. Two women at a café described cockatoos as "sassy." What does this word mean?

   a. Rude and showing no respect
   b. Smart and well-behaved
   c. Cute and charming

3. Who saw two cockatoos pulling the rubber lining out of the cars?

   a. Isaac Sherring-Tito, a Katoomba resident
   b. Sophie Miller, an artist
   c. Mel Jones, a café owner

PHASE 4

💬✅ Output Task (Writing / Speaking)

Step 1 ▶ Answer the following questions.

a. Do you like sulphur-crested cockatoos? Why?

e.g., Yes, I do because they are very funny and friendly to people.

b. Do you want to keep one as a pet? Why?

e.g., No, I don't because I want to keep my apartment clean.

Step 2 Ask a partner the questions from the previous page and complete the sentences below.

a. My partner, _____, said that he/she _____
(your partner's name)   likes sulphur-crested cockatoos

because _____.
they are very intelligent

b. He/She said that he/she _____
wants to keep one as a pet

This is because _____
he/she is excited to see the cockatoo's smart and creative behaviors

_____.

Step 3 Practice the report that you made in Step 2. Then, present the report to the class.

Checklist for the Presentation

Use this checklist to evaluate one of your classmate's presentations.

		Good				Bad
1.	The speaker speaks clearly.	5	4	3	2	1
2.	The speaker speaks in correct sentence forms.	5	4	3	2	1
3.	The speaker gives clear reasons for his/her partner's statement.	5	4	3	2	1
4.	The speaker makes eye contact with the audience.	5	4	3	2	1

How to Become a Good Journalist

Have you ever been interested in journalism? According to Katharine Viner, the editor-in-chief at *the Guardian*, it seems that there are some important things you need to know to be a good journalist. What are they?

PHASE 1

1 | Getting into the Topic

Read the short article, and fill in the blanks with the appropriate words from below.

Guardian sees digital readers
[1](   ) **sharply over the past year**

While print [2](   ) are on the decline across the newspaper industry, *the Guardian*, one of the UK's [3](   ) newspapers, gained 268,000 new digital [2](   ) during the year 2020. This was a 43% [1](   ) since 2019.

| leading | subscriptions | increase |

33

2 | ▪◀ 1st Viewing

online / video

Watch the video and choose the best answers to the following questions.

1. How does Katharine Viner look?
   a. She looks like she's enjoying her job.
   b. She looks like she's tired of her job.
   c. She looks like she's worried about her job.

2. How many questions does Viner answer?
   a. Two
   b. Three
   c. Four

PHASE 2

1 | 📋 Vocabulary

Match the words with their definitions.

1. **conservative** ☐

2. **investigate** ☐

3. **expose** ☐

4. **accountable** ☐

5. **rewarding** ☐

a. making you feel happy because you feel that you are doing something useful

b. to show something to the public

c. to try to find out how things happened or what is the truth

d. responsible for something

e. unwilling to change and accept new ideas

2 📖 Reading

Read the following passage.

 DL 10   CD 10

Inside a UK's Leading Newspaper Company

The Guardian, one of the UK's most popular daily newspapers, started as a weekly paper in Manchester (in the north of England) in 1821. The Guardian Media Group, whose members include *the Observer*, the oldest newspaper still running in Britain, now has more than one million subscribers around the world. *The Guardian* is less
5 conservative than the UK's other main newspapers and is famous for its investigative journalism. It prides itself on "giving a voice to the powerless" in society.

It takes many people to produce a newspaper such as *the Guardian*. *The Guardian*'s first female editor-in-chief, Katharine Viner, explains that in addition to employing the reporters who write articles, *the Guardian* employs editors, designers,
10 and engineers. The editors are the people who decide which stories are written. They send reporters out to investigate stories, then check them for accuracy. Designers make each page look balanced and organized. Finally, engineers make all of the articles work properly on our smartphones and computers.

According to Viner, the best part of her role is publishing an important story,
15 such as exposing a lying politician. She describes it as "holding people accountable for what they do," which is necessary to change the world for the better.

She says that to be a good journalist, the most important thing is to be curious about the world. Being a good writer is the second most important thing. The best writers communicate their stories to the public using clear and simple language. Now,
20 are you interested in getting a job in journalism? Viner's words fully describe how rewarding the job of a journalist could be!   (269 words)

Notes

ℓ2 **Manchester:** one of the UK's most famous cities, situated in the north-western part of England

ℓ3 ***The Observer*:** A British newspaper published on Sundays, which is the world's oldest Sunday Newspaper. It began in 1791 and became part of the Guardian Media Group in 1993.

3 | 📄 Summary

 🎧 DL 11   ⊙ CD 11

Fill in the blanks and complete the summary of the reading.

It takes a great many people to produce a newspaper such as *the Guardian*, one of the UK's (**l** _____) daily newspapers. According to *the Guardian*'s first female editor-in-chief, Katharine Viner, there are two (**i** _____) things that make a good journalist. One is being (**c** _____) about the world, and the other is being a good writer who can (**c** _____) his or her stories to the public using (**c** _____) and simple language.

PHASE 3

◼◀ 2nd Viewing

(online / video)

Watch the video again and choose the best answers to the following questions.

1. As the editor-in-chief at *the Guardian*, what is Katharine Viner NOT responsible for?

   a. Their office building maintenance
   b. Exposing politicians who are telling lies
   c. *The Guardian*'s newspapers

2. According to Viner, when is a politician considered to have "lied?"

   a. When he/she has got a big story
   b. When he/she said one thing and did another
   c. When he/she changed the world for the better

3. What does good journalism mean to Viner?

   a. To build a fair society
   b. To help politicians lie
   c. To make people interested in what is happening

PHASE 4

💬✔ **Output Task** (Writing / Speaking)

Step I ▶ Answer the following questions.

a. What kind of job do you want to get in the future?

e.g., I want to be an elementary school teacher.

....

....

b. Why do you want to get that job?

e.g., Because I like children and I think that the job is rewarding.

....

....

c. What do you think is necessary to get the job? Write at least two things.

e.g., To be an elementary school teacher, I think that it is necessary to be friendly to children. I also think that it is necessary to know a lot of things.

....

....

....

Beginner

Step 2 Ask a partner the questions from the previous page and complete the sentences below.

a. My partner, _____, wants to be _____

(your partner's name)   a doctor

b. because _____

he/she is interested in medicine and he/she wants to help people

_____.

c. He/She thinks that to be _____, it is necessary to _____

                                     a doctor   gain a lot of

_____ and to _____

knowledge about medicine   be able to listen to

_____.

those in need

Step 3 Practice the report that you made in Step 2. Then, present the report to the class.

Checklist for the Presentation

Use this checklist to evaluate one of your classmate's presentations.

Good ... Bad

1. The speaker speaks clearly.   5 4 3 2 1

2. The speaker speaks in correct sentence forms.   5 4 3 2 1

3. The speaker gives clear reasons for his/her partner's statement.   5 4 3 2 1

4. The speaker makes eye contact with the audience.   5 4 3 2 1

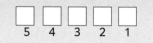

Universal Credit: Helping or Hurting the Poor?

The problem of poverty is becoming more serious, and governments around the world are trying to help the poor. One way the UK has tried is Universal Credit (UC). What is UC? Does it help low-income families?

PHASE 1

1 | Getting into the Topic

Fill in the blanks with the appropriate words from below to complete the brief explanation of "Universal Credit."

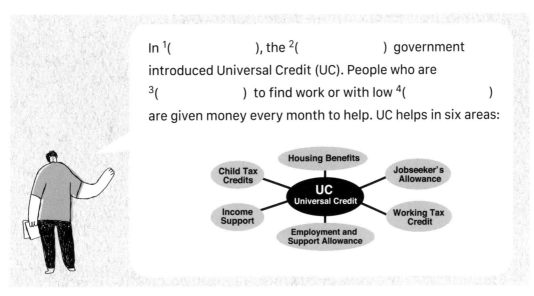

In ¹(   ), the ²(   ) government introduced Universal Credit (UC). People who are ³(   ) to find work or with low ⁴(   ) are given money every month to help. UC helps in six areas:

Housing Benefits

Child Tax Credits

Jobseeker's Allowance

UC
Universal Credit

Income Support

Working Tax Credit

Employment and Support Allowance

| UK | income | 2013 | struggling |

Beginner

2 | ◼◀ 1st Viewing

online/video

Watch the video and choose the best answers to the following questions.

1. How is Trent Seymour after the start of Universal Credit (UC)?

   a. Poor
   b. Happy
   c. No problem

2. What percentage of people in UC areas use food banks?

   a. 13%
   b. 39%
   c. 52%

PHASE 2

1 | 📋 Vocabulary

Match the words with their definitions.

1. delay

a. to try hard to do something even though it is difficult

2. apply for

b. a period of time when somebody must wait because of a problem that makes something slow

3. struggle

c. the state of owing money

4. debt

d. opportunities to do something; space

5. room

e. to make a formal request for something such as a job, money, or permission to do something

2 📖 Reading

Read the following passage.

 DL 12   CD 12

Universal Credit: A Success or a Nightmare?

Universal Credit (UC) is a pretty new social security system in the UK. It started in 2013. It is money that the government gives to low-income families. Before UC, there were six different payments for different problems. For example, there was one payment for the unemployed and another payment for the homeless. Prime Minister
5 Theresa May said that UC, which combines all those payments, was "an important reform" and "a simpler system."

However, due to many hassles with the transition to the new system, many problems occurred when UC was first started. The main problem was that there was a long delay between applying for UC and receiving the money. In some cases, people
10 had to wait 12 weeks for their first payment, meaning they could not pay their rent on time and had to take out loans. Some people even lost their homes.

Trent Seymour, a man on UC, said that the new system was a nightmare. He was struggling to pay his phone bills or buy food, and the delay in receiving UC had put him into debt. Food bank staff member Charlotte Hughes said the number of food
15 bank users had increased. Her colleague, Colin Marchbank-Smith, agreed that UC was making poverty worse. He had seen people who had not eaten for days.

Jeremy Corbyn, who was the Labour Party leader until 2020, told Theresa May to "pause Universal Credit and fix the problems" with the system. However, May did not do this. She said UC should continue. Maybe UC is not a bad system, but it is not
20 working. The idea of UC is simpler than six different payments, but there is a lot of room for improvement.

(266 words)

Notes

ℓ 1 **social security:** government money that is paid to people who are unemployed, old, ill, etc.

ℓ 5 **Theresa May:** a former Prime Minister of the UK (2016-2019)

ℓ 14 **food bank:** a place where food and groceries are given for free to people who need them

ℓ 17 **Labour Party:** one of the main political parties in the UK

Beginner

3 📄 Summary 🎧 DL 13   ⊙ CD 13

Fill in the blanks and complete the summary of the reading.

Universal Credit (UC) is a relatively new social security payment that low-income (**f**   ) in the UK can receive. However, many problems (**o**   ) when UC was first started. One of the biggest problems was that there was a long (**d**   ) between applying for UC and receiving the money. The (**i**   ) of UC itself may be essentially good, but there seems to be a lot of (**r**   ) for improvement in terms of how it works.

PHASE 3

🎞 2nd Viewing

Watch the video again and choose the best answers to the following questions.

1. What does Jeremy Corbyn, the male politician in a suit, think about UC?

   a. He thinks that UC should be paused until it is fixed.
   b. He thinks that UC is a good way to help people in poverty and should be continued as planned.
   c. He thinks the number of UC payments should be increased.

2. Colin Marchbank-Smith says, "That's not pretence. That's reality." What does he mean?

   a. The problems with UC will be solved soon.
   b. People are actually struggling.
   c. The idea of UC is good.

3. How many families in the UK are in trouble due to issues with UC?

   a. 28, 000
   b. 280,000
   c. 2,800,000

PHASE 4

💬✍ Output Task (Writing / Speaking)

Step 1 ▶ Answer the following questions.

a. UC in the UK had a lot of problems when it was first introduced. Do some research on the reasons why it did not work well and write down the reason that you think is most important.

> e.g., It takes a long time for the government to decide how much UC a person gets.

....
....

b. What do you think the UK should do to help people in need?

> e.g., I think that the UK should create a better system of UC to help people in need.

....
....

Step 2 Ask a partner the questions from the previous page and complete the sentences below.

a. According to my partner _____, one reason why UC payments
(your partner's name)

are delayed is that _____

_____.

b. He/She thinks that the UK should _____

_____.

Step 3 Practice the report that you made in Step 2. Then, present the report to the class.

Checklist for the Presentation

Use this checklist to evaluate one of your classmate's presentations.

		Good				Bad
1.	The speaker speaks clearly.	5	4	3	2	1
2.	The speaker speaks in correct sentence forms.	5	4	3	2	1
3.	The speaker explains his/her partner's idea clearly.	5	4	3	2	1
4.	The speaker makes eye contact with the audience.	5	4	3	2	1

UNIT 7

Cooling is Heating?

Air conditioning is used everywhere. It is almost impossible for us to live without air conditioning today. However, our use of air conditioning is said to be one cause of a difficult problem. Do you really think that air conditioning helps us feel cooler?

PHASE 1

1 | Getting into the Topic

The following is a ranking of electricity consumption by country in 2019. Guess which countries from below fit blanks 1–5.

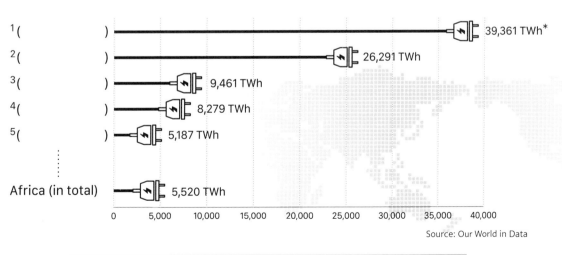

¹ (   ) ———————————————— 39,361 TWh*

² (   ) ———————————— 26,291 TWh

³ (   ) ———— 9,461 TWh

⁴ (   ) ——— 8,279 TWh

⁵ (   ) —— 5,187 TWh

Africa (in total) — 5,520 TWh

0   5,000   10,000   15,000   20,000   25,000   30,000   35,000   40,000

Source: Our World in Data

India	The US	Japan	China	Russia

*TWh: terawatt-hour (one TWh = energy equal to outputting one trillion watts for one hour)

45

2 | ⬛◀ 1st Viewing

online video

Watch the video and choose the best answers to the following questions.

1. In which country do nearly 90% of households use electricity for air conditioning?
   a. China
   b. India
   c. The United States

2. How many tons of food is the world currently wasting?
   a. 13,000,000
   b. 130,000,000
   c. 1,300,000,000

PHASE 2

1 | 📋 Vocabulary

Match the words with their definitions.

1. **chill** ☐

2. **enormous** ☐

3. **emissions** ☐

4. **ironic** ☐

5. **crucial** ☐

a. an amount of gas, heat, or light that is sent out into the air

b. describing a situation in which something opposite to what was expected happens

c. extremely important or necessary

d. to make something cool

e. very large in size, volume, or area

2 📖 Reading

Read the following passage.

 DL 14 CD 14

Does Cooling Down Heat Up the Planet?

Modern life would not be possible without air conditioners, refrigerators, and freezers. These machines cool our homes, cars, and offices, and chill our food and medicines. Air conditioning is a pretty modern invention and it only really started to become essential to our lives in the 1990s. In fact, in 1990, there were only around
5 400 million air conditioning units in the world. Now, there are believed to be over 1.9 billion units in the world. In the US, around 87% of households have air conditioning.

Why is this a problem? The main reason is that it requires an enormous amount of electricity. In fact, the amount of electricity used for air conditioners in the US is greater than Africa's total electricity output. Generating electricity causes carbon
10 dioxide emissions, which are responsible for global warming. It is sad and ironic that cooling our homes is heating the planet.

At the same time, cooling technology is crucial for people in developing countries. Many of them live in rural areas far from the main market and do not have enough food. If refrigerated trucks delivered fresh food to them, it could potentially feed one
15 billion more people in the world. That means that we could also save millions of tons of food that the world is currently wasting.

How do we solve this difficult problem? The answer is clean energy. We must give up "dirty" energy like oil and coal and find ways to generate electricity in an environmentally friendly way. That means trying to use more electricity generated
20 from renewable sources, such as hydro, wind, and solar energy.   (267 words)

Notes

ℓ 9 **carbon dioxide:** the gas formed when carbon is burned or when people or animals breathe out; CO₂

ℓ 20 **hydro energy:** a form of energy that uses the power of moving water to generate electricity

3 📄 Summary

Fill in the blanks and complete the summary of the reading.

Modern life would be (**i**   ) without air conditioning, but cooling is said to be a problem. The main reason is that it requires an (**e**   ) amount of electricity. Generating electricity creates carbon dioxide (**e**   ), which contribute to global warming. However, cooling technology is (**c**   ) for people, especially in developing countries. The answer to solve this problem is to use (**c**   ) energy, such as hydro, wind, and solar energy.

PHASE 3

◼◀ 2nd Viewing

Watch the video again and choose the best answers to the following questions.

1. In the video, the narrator says "cold is dirty." What does that mean?

   a. You need a large amount of oil and coal to make air conditioning units.
   b. The insides of air conditioning units are very dirty.
   c. The ways we cool things now lead to polluting the environment.

2. What is said about airplanes?

   a. Airplanes are very useful to send air conditioning units overseas.
   b. Airplanes generate emissions, too, but not as much as air conditioning.
   c. Airplanes need to have a lot of air conditioning units.

3. By when is it said that the global use of air conditioning for cooling will overtake that for heating?

   a. 2030
   b. 2060
   c. 2100

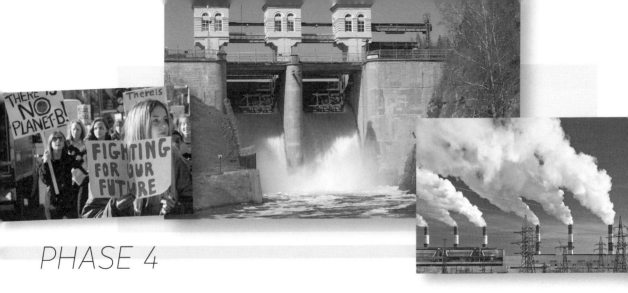

PHASE 4

💬✍ **Output Task** (Writing / Speaking)

Step 1 ▶ Answer the following questions.

a. Which clean energy solution are you interested in the most? Choose one.

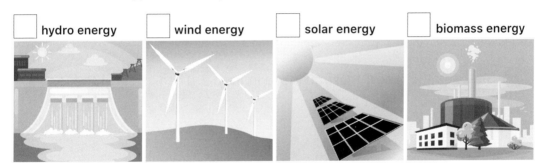

| ☐ **hydro energy** | ☐ **wind energy** | ☐ **solar energy** | ☐ **biomass energy** |

b. Do some research on the advantages of the clean energy you chose and write down one of them.

> e.g., An advantage of hydro energy is that it is highly efficient in energy conversion.

....
....

c. Do some research on the disadvantages of the same clean energy and write down one of them.

> e.g., A disadvantage of hydro energy is that it costs a lot to build power plants.

....
....

Step 2 Ask a partner the questions from the previous page and complete the sentences below.

a. My partner, _____, is interested in _____
(your partner's name)   solar

energy.

b. According to him/her, an advantage of _____ energy is that
                                          solar

_____ ,
solar panels can be placed anywhere

c. but a disadvantage of _____ energy is that _____
                          solar   the amount of energy

_____ .
supply depends on the weather

Step 3 Practice the report that you made in Step 2. Then, present the report to the class.

Checklist for the Presentation

Use this checklist to evaluate one of your classmate's presentations.

		Good				Bad
1.	The speaker speaks clearly.	5	4	3	2	1
2.	The speaker speaks in correct sentence forms.	5	4	3	2	1
3.	The speaker explains both an advantage and a disadvantage.	5	4	3	2	1
4.	The speaker makes eye contact with the audience.	5	4	3	2	1

Fashion's Resale Revolution

Have you ever bought secondhand clothes? Recently, more and more young people want them, but why are young people interested in secondhand? What are some popular ways to get these clothes?

PHASE 1

1 | Getting into the Topic

Look at the graph that shows what European people (16–75 years old) think about clothes. Choose T (True) or F (False) for each sentence.

✏ **How many people say they ...**

■ Wear clothes for at least a few years	62%
■ Pass on unwanted clothes to someone else to use	53%
■ Wash clothes only when dirty	48%
■ Always wash clothes after wearing once	17%
■ Avoid buying new clothes	9%

Source: Fashion Revolution Foundation 2020

1. About 60% say they throw away their clothes within a few years after buying them.

   [T / F]

2. More than half of the people give their unwanted clothes to someone else. [T / F]

3. There are more people who always wash their clothes after wearing once than people who wash their clothes only when dirty. [T / F]

51

2 ◀ 1st Viewing

online video

Watch the video and choose the best answers to the following questions.

1. Where do the first two men buy their clothes?
   a. On the Internet
   b. At charity shops
   c. At auction

2. Who is Isabella Vrana?
   a. A successful seller on a fashion marketplace app
   b. An interviewer
   c. A staff member at a charity shop

PHASE 2

1 Vocabulary

Match the words with their definitions.

1. **retail** ☐	**a.** something that makes something move forward
2. **driver** ☐	**b.** a number that is 100,000 or more, especially an amount of money
3. **six figures** ☐	**c.** the selling of goods to the public, usually through shops
4. **platform** ☐	**d.** the type of computer system or software that someone uses
5. **resonate** ☐	**e.** to be similar to what somebody thinks or believes

Read the following passage.   DL 16   CD 16

The Secondhand Boom

In Britain, attitudes toward buying and wearing secondhand clothes have changed. Now, 43% of Britons have bought used clothes and 24% are interested in doing so. In fact, the market for used clothes has recently grown 21 times faster than the retail market.

5 There are three main reasons why buying used clothes is becoming so popular. First, thanks to social media, young people are being photographed more than ever before and want a greater variety of clothing in order to change their look. Buying secondhand clothes means they can easily change their wardrobes. Second, young people are more aware of sustainability in fashion. Third, secondhand clothing is
10 usually cheaper than new clothing. Many young people want designer or branded clothing, and it is cheaper to buy these secondhand.

Where do young people buy secondhand clothes? Many people shop at secondhand clothing stores and charity shops. However, the biggest drivers of the used clothes market are apps, such as Depop. Depop is a shopping app, but it is also
15 a kind of social media tool. Buyers can "like" and "follow" sellers that interest them. Top sellers on Depop can earn up to six figures. One top seller, Isabella Vrana, says she is successful because she sells clothes that she actually likes and wears. Her store's popularity shows how the platform is bringing buyers and sellers together. One fashion retail expert says that today, people want to buy from somebody they can
20 "resonate with," rather than from big stores.

In a world where image is important and variety is everything, the secondhand clothing trend seems to be here to stay.   (268 words)

Notes

ℓ 2 **Briton:** a person from Britain

ℓ 14 **Depop:** a fashion marketplace app started in London, UK in 2011

Beginner

3 📄 Summary 🎧 DL 17 ⊙ CD 17

Fill in the blanks and complete the summary of the reading.

In Britain, the market for (**s**   ) clothes has been popular among

young people. There are three main reasons: their desire for variety, their awareness

about (**s**   ) in fashion, and the low prices of used clothes. Young

people use (**a**   ), such as Depop, when buying and reselling used

clothes. The secondhand clothing (**t**   ) seems to be here to

(**s**   ).

PHASE 3

◼◀ 2nd Viewing

Watch the video again and choose the best answers to the following
questions.

1. What are StockX, Goat, Grailed, Vestiaire Collective, and The RealReal?

  a. Names of retail stores
  b. Names of charity shops
  c. Names of shopping apps

2. What did the video suggest was a problem with online stores in the old days?

  a. Online stores in the old days were slow and didn't look nice.
  b. Everything in online stores was very expensive.
  c. Only a very limited number of people had access to the online stores at a time.

3. What kind of clothes does Isabella sell on Depop?

  a. The coolest clothes
  b. Very expensive clothes
  c. Clothes that she likes

PHASE 4

💬✍️ Output Task (Writing / Speaking)

Step 1 ▶ Answer the following questions.

a. Where do you usually buy your clothes from? Why?

e.g., I usually buy my clothes on the Internet because I don't have to go out.

b. Which do you prefer, new clothes or secondhand clothes? Why?

e.g., I prefer secondhand clothes because they are cheaper than new clothes.

c. Do you want to sell your clothes on the Internet? Why or why not?

e.g., Yes, I do because I want to get money by selling clothes that I don't wear.

Step 2 Ask a partner the questions from the previous page and complete the sentences below.

a. My partner, _____, usually buys his/her clothes _____
(your partner's name)   at clothes stores

because _____ .
he/she wants to try them on before buying them

b. He/She prefers _____ clothes because _____
new   he/she doesn't want to wear clothes

_____ .
that someone has worn

c. He/She _____
doesn't want to sell his/her clothes on the Internet

because _____ .
they are all special to him/her

Step 3 Practice the report that you made in Step 2. Then, present the report to the class.

Checklist for the Presentation

Use this checklist to evaluate one of your classmate's presentations.

		Good				Bad
1.	The speaker speaks clearly.	5	4	3	2	1
2.	The speaker speaks in correct sentence forms.	5	4	3	2	1
3.	The speaker gives clear reasons for his/her partner's statement.	5	4	3	2	1
4.	The speaker makes eye contact with the audience.	5	4	3	2	1

Finding Treasures in the Trash

There is a proverb in English, "One man's trash is another man's treasure." It means that something that one person thinks is worthless may be valuable to someone else. What is your treasure? Is it something expensive or well-known? Why is it a treasure to you?

PHASE 1

1 | Getting into the Topic

Read the descriptions of the items sold on an online flea market and fill in the blanks with the appropriate words from below.

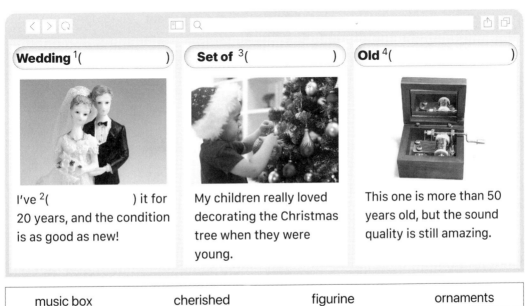

| Wedding ¹( ) | Set of ³( ) | Old ⁴( ) |

I've ²( ) it for 20 years, and the condition is as good as new!

My children really loved decorating the Christmas tree when they were young.

This one is more than 50 years old, but the sound quality is still amazing.

| music box | cherished | figurine | ornaments |

2 📹 1st Viewing

online video

Watch the video and choose the best answers to the following questions.

1. What is this place?
   a. An antique shop
   b. A grocery store
   c. A trash museum

2. What is this person's job?
   a. Fireman
   b. Sanitation worker
   c. Shop clerk

PHASE 2

1 📋 Vocabulary

Match the words with their definitions.

1. decade ☐

a. matters, materials, or objects whose names are not important

2. mere ☐

b. a small worthless object used for decoration

3. stuff ☐

c. a period of ten years

4. knickknack ☐

d. only

5. cherish ☐

e. to love, protect, and care for

2 📖 Reading

Read the following passage.

 DL 18   CD 18

Treasures in the Trash:
The Amazing Things New Yorkers Throw Away

The second floor of the New York City Department of Sanitation building in East Harlem is home to thousands of objects that New Yorkers have thrown away over the last three decades. These items were found in the trash. They are actually old, but do not look like mere garbage. They have been carefully cleaned, organized, and kept by
5 a sanitation worker, Nelson Molina.

Molina has worked for the Sanitation Department for 34 years and started collecting these items about 29 years ago. Since then, he and his coworkers have collected many items while doing their daily jobs and have stored the items here. "We're not allowed to take stuff home," Molina said. "That's why I like to display and
10 everything."

Molina calls this place "The Museum" although it is not yet open to the public. In The Museum, there is a wide variety of old items, such as figurines, pictures, knickknacks, silent movies, projectors, and much more. One thing Molina cherishes here is a little Star of David made of the steel from the World Trade Center building.
15 He says it is a treasure to him.

Molina is going to retire from his sanitation job soon. However, he lives only 15 blocks away from the Sanitation building, so he will be coming to The Museum often to check on his treasures. He hopes that the Sanitation Department keeps the collection in this building, fixes the building, and opens The Museum to the public.

(244 words)

Notes

ℓ 1 **East Harlem:** the northeastern part of Manhattan; one of the largest Hispanic communities in New York City

ℓ 13 **silent movie (also known as silent film):** a type of movie with no sound or speech made by the actors

ℓ 14 **Star of David:** a six-pointed star, made with two overlaid triangles, used as a symbol for the Jewish religion; found in the center of the Israeli flag

ℓ 14 **World Trade Center:** a large group of buildings in the southwest of Manhattan which were destroyed in terrorist attacks on September 11, 2001

3 | 📄 Summary

🎧 DL 19   💿 CD 19

Fill in the blanks and complete the summary of the reading.

Nelson Molina, a sanitation worker in New York, has collected a lot of items from

the (**t**   ) for about three decades. He now (**d**   )

them in a trash museum. These items include figurines, pictures, knickknacks,

silent movies, and more. Among them, he especially (**c**   ) a little

Star of David as his (**t**   ). He wants the museum to remain here

and be opened to the (**p**   ).

PHASE 3

🔊 2nd Viewing

(online video)

Watch the video again and choose the best answers to the following questions.

1. What is special about the officers' picture?

    a. Everybody in the picture signed it.
    b. There are 1,944 officers in it.
    c. Molina found it in the trash in 1944.

2. In order to see the collection in the museum, what should a visitor do?

    a. Call New York City and get authorization
    b. Explain to Molina what they want to see
    c. Donate a treasure of their own to the museum

3. When will Molina retire?

    a. In 6 months
    b. In 8 months
    c. In 15 months

PHASE 4

💬✍ Output Task (Writing / Speaking)

Step 1 ▶ Answer the following questions.

a. What is your treasure?

e.g., I have a good luck charm attached to my bag. It is my treasure.

b. How did you get it?

e.g., It was a souvenir from my grandfather.

c. Why is it your treasure?

e.g., He bought it at Dazaifu Tenmangu, wishing that I would pass the entrance exam and I did!
I appreciate his kindness and still cherish the charm now.

Step 2 Ask a partner the questions from the previous page and complete the sentences below.

a. My partner _____'s treasure is _____
(your partner's name)   a yellow coffee mug. He/She uses it at

_____ .
home

b. He/She got it [/It was] _____ .
when he/she traveled to Matsue, Shimane Prefecture

c. He/She _____
loved it when he/she first saw it at a pottery gallery. He/She likes its round-bottom shape and

_____ .
uses it for morning coffee every day

Step 3 Practice the report that you made in Step 2. Then, present the report to the class.

Checklist for the Presentation

Use this checklist to evaluate one of your classmate's presentations.

		Good				Bad
1.	The speaker speaks clearly.	5	4	3	2	1
2.	The speaker speaks in correct sentence forms.	5	4	3	2	1
3.	he speaker talks about the story behind his/her partner's treasure.	5	4	3	2	1
4.	The speaker makes eye contact with the audience.	5	4	3	2	1

Climate Protesters Going to Prison

Climate change has become a serious global issue. Nowadays, people around the world have started to take action against this problem— some make speeches in public and others participate in strikes or marches. Are there any other ways to protest?

PHASE 1

1 | Getting into the Topic

Read about famous protests in recent years and choose the best option that fits blanks A–C from below.

A. (   )
Protests against income inequality in the US, which began on September 17, 2011 around Zuccotti Park in Manhattan, New York

B. (   )
Racial protests in the US in response to police violence against African Americans, such as George Floyd

C. (   )
School strikes for climate change, launched by Swedish environmental activist Greta Thunberg

| Fridays for Future | Black Lives Matter | Occupy Wall Street |

2 | 🎥◀ 1st Viewing

online video

Watch the video and choose the best answers to the following questions.

1. Who are the people speaking loudly?
   a. Police officers
   b. Protesters
   c. Politicians

2. What are they worrying about?
   a. Global warming
   b. War
   c. Discrimination

PHASE 2

1 | 📋 Vocabulary

Match the words with their definitions.

1. **extinction** ☐

   a. a situation in which animals or plants no longer exist

2. **address** ☐

   b. not doing anything even though doing something is expected or appropriate

3. **protest** ☐

   c. to intentionally not listen to or pay attention to something

4. **inaction** ☐

   d. to express disagreement, often by shouting, carrying signs, etc.

5. **ignore** ☐

   e. to think about or begin to do something to solve an issue or a problem

2 📖 Reading

Read the following passage.

We Will Go to Prison for This Planet!

Life on Earth is facing extinction due to global warming. According to a UN report, as of 2018, we had 12 years left to avoid a climate change catastrophe. This means that unless we take a huge step to address climate change by 2030, there will be no turning back!

5　　In the face of this crisis, people around the world have started to protest against the governments' inaction on climate change. Among them, a group of activists called Extinction Rebellion have started a campaign of civil disobedience across London.

"We can stop climate change by going to prison," says one activist, Ian Bray, who is worried about the future for his two children. "I'm far more afraid of climate
10　change than I am of arrest and imprisonment."

One woman shouts, "I'm willing to go to prison for this planet, and I'm willing to go again and again and again until I see some results, until we all see a better world!"

They intentionally get arrested by the police and go to prison in order to raise public awareness and call for government policies on climate change. The Extinction
15　Rebellion activists hope that their personal sacrifices will move the government and make the world a better place.

Bray sees climate change as an existential threat and worries that people are all going to die if they continue to ignore this problem. He says, "This is partly an attempt to start behaving as if it's an emergency." He hopes that more people will start
20　acting to solve this problem.　　　　　　　　　　　　　　　　　　(257 words)

Notes

ℓ 7　**Extinction Rebellion:** a global movement that aims to protect the environment without using violence

ℓ 7　**civil disobedience:** the act of refusing to obey rules or laws in order to protest against the government without using violence

ℓ 17　**existential threat:** something that is likely to cause damage or danger to someone's existence or life

3 | 📄 Summary

🎧 DL 21    CD 21

Fill in the blanks and complete the summary of the reading.

In the face of the climate change (**c**   ), a group of activists

called Extinction Rebellion have started a campaign of civil disobedience in

London. By intentionally getting (**a**   ) by the police and going to

(**p**   ), they aim to raise public (**a**   ) about

climate change and call for new government (**p**   ). They also

want other people to tackle this problem.

PHASE 3

▶ 2nd Viewing

online/video

Watch the video again and choose the best answers to the following
questions.

1. Genny Scherer put a small note on a door window that says, "GLUED ON.
   Don't Try To Move." What does this message mean?

   a. She has a strong intention to stay where she is.
   b. She is going to glue the note onto the glass.
   c. She needs help because she is glued and cannot move.

2. The video text says, "Activists say 'we must increase pressure.'" What/Who is being
   pressured?

   a. Climate change
   b. The government
   c. The police

3. Which of the followings is NOT a form of nonviolent protest that the activists in the
   video showed?

   a. Fighting with police officers
   b. Spraying paint on a wall or window
   c. Standing and blocking the entrance of a building

PHASE 4

💬✍ Output Task (Writing / Speaking)

Step 1 ▶ In the video, the Extinction Rebellion activists sprayed paint on a wall, lay in the street, and blocked the entrance to a building. Answer the following questions.

a. Do you like their campaign? Why?

> e.g., I like their campaign because civil disobedience campaigns have a good effect on society. /
> I don't like their campaign because their behavior is against the morals of society.

I _____ because _____

_____ .

b. What kind of social movement do you want to participate in? Why?

Kind of social movement	 e.g., A campaign to close the gap between the rich and the poor
Reason	 e.g., Because I strongly feel that the gap between the rich and the poor is serious

Step 2 Ask a partner the questions from the previous page and complete the sentences below.

a. My partner, _____ , _____ the Extinction Rebellion campaign
  (your partner's name)   likes

  because he/she _____ .
          thinks that its activities will surely raise awareness for climate change

b. He/She wants to participate in a campaign _____
                  to reduce marine plastic waste

c. because he/she _____ .
        is worried that it has a negative impact on sea animals

Step 3 Practice the report that you made in Step 2. Then, present the report to the class.

Checklist for the Presentation

Use this checklist to evaluate one of your classmate's presentations.

		Good				Bad
1.	The speaker speaks clearly.	5	4	3	2	1
2.	The speaker speaks in correct sentence forms.	5	4	3	2	1
3.	The speaker gives clear reasons for his/her partner's statement.	5	4	3	2	1
4.	The speaker makes eye contact with the audience.	5	4	3	2	1

UNIT 11

The Changing Meaning of "Home"

The way people think about "home" seems to be changing these days. This is a story about a couple who have an interesting opinion about it. They use Airbnb to change where they live once a month. What does "home" mean to you?

PHASE 1

1 Getting into the Topic

Read the information from an online accommodation booking site. Fill in the blanks with the appropriate words below.

APARTMENT

Long-term Guest Apartment
—*month to month*

Manhattan, New York, United States

▶ 2 guests ▶ 1 bedroom ▶ 1 bed ▶ 1 bath
▶ $3,300/month

Situated in an exciting [1](   ) in NYC, this apartment is perfect for your monthly stay! It is fully equipped with [2](   ). The kitchen is well [3](   ), with a fridge, a microwave oven, pans, and a set of dishes! Free Wi-Fi and air conditioning are also [4](   ).

furniture	stocked	available	neighborhood

Beginner

2 | 1st Viewing

Watch the video and choose the best answers to the following questions.

1. How does the couple look?

   a. Angry

   b. Happy

   c. Serious

2. How does Robert feel about the video shop?

   a. Great

   b. Weird

   c. Terrible

PHASE 2

1 | Vocabulary

Match the words with their definitions.

1. settle in

2. accommodation

3. nostalgic

4. liken

5. physical

a. feeling pleasant and also slightly sad when you remember a good time in the past

b. buildings or rooms where people live, work, or stay

c. to say that one thing is similar to another

d. to start living in a place

e. describing that something actually exists and can be seen and felt

2 📖 Reading

Read the following passage.

 DL 22   CD 22

No Fixed Home, No Fixed Lifestyle

How would you like to move house every so often? Well, one couple has been doing this for a while. American couple David Roberts and Elaine Kuok decided to settle in New York after living in various locations around the world. However, instead of buying their own home, they chose to live in Airbnb accommodations for
5 a month at a time, each in a different neighborhood.

What is the couple's lifestyle like? They keep their belongings to a minimum, filling just three suitcases between them, because everything they need for their daily lives is provided by Airbnb. David and Elaine enjoy the fact that they can experience living in different neighborhoods. David says that he likes to build up a relationship
10 with each neighborhood. Whenever they return and see the coffee shops they had visited before or the video shops they had browsed in, they feel nostalgic. He likens the experience to dating. He says, "It's almost like we've dated this person a little bit, right? And so we know these neighborhoods in a slightly different way than if [we] hadn't lived there for a month or two."

15 Some people may find such a lifestyle unusual, but the idea of "home" is actually changing. Vicky Richardson, an architecture expert, points out that for more and more people, "home" is where you can connect with your online profile. It is no longer a physical place with material objects. The Internet has changed the way we work, but will it change the way we live, too? It might become
20 normal to live like David and Elaine in the near future.

(268 words)

Notes

ℓ 4   **Airbnb**[éə bi: en bí:]: an online marketplace founded in 2008 that connects people who want to rent out their homes with people who are looking for accommodation in specific areas

3 📄 Summary

 🎧 DL 23   ⏺ CD 23

Fill in the blanks and complete the summary of the reading.

David Roberts and Elaine Kuok have been living in Airbnb (**a**   )

for a while. Everything they need for their daily lives is provided by

(**A**   ), so they can keep their (**b**   ) to a minimum.

Like David and Elaine, it seems that people these days have a different idea of what

"(**h**   )" is. An architecture expert points out that for more and

more people, home is no longer a (**p**   ) place with material

objects. This idea might become normal in the near future.

PHASE 3

⏺◀ 2nd Viewing

online / video

Watch the video again and choose the best answers to the following questions.

1. How long have David and Elaine been married?

    a. For about a year and a half

    b. For 14 years

    c. For more than 15 years

2. Why did David and Elaine start living in Airbnb accommodations?

    a. David wanted to see if it was possible to live in a different neighborhood every month without making a permanent home.

    b. They thought that it would be cheaper to stay in Airbnb accommodations than buying their own house.

    c. They had experience working for Airbnb.

3. According to Vicky Richardson, what is the "digital bubble" like?

    a. Because of it, we can travel around the world easily.

    b. Because of it, our worlds are getting smaller and more connected.

    c. Because of it, we cannot live in conventional homes.

PHASE 4

💬✏️ **Output Task** (Writing / Speaking)

Step 1 ▶ Answer the following questions.

a. What do you think about David and Elaine's lifestyle with Airbnb?

e.g., I think that their lifestyle with Airbnb is attractive.

....

....

b. Why do you think so?

e.g., Because they can enjoy living in a lot of places.

....

....

c. What does "home" mean to you?

e.g., To me, "home" means where I can use Wi-Fi and get as much information as I want.

....

....

Step 2 Ask a partner the questions from the previous page and complete the sentences below.

a. My partner, _____, thinks that David and Elaine's lifestyle with
   (your partner's name)

   Airbnb is _____
            stressful

b. because _____ .
           it often takes time to get used to a new place

c. To him/her, "home" means _____
                          where he/she can relax and spend time with his/her family

   _____ .

Step 3 Practice the report that you made in Step 2. Then, present the report to the class.

Checklist for the Presentation

Use this checklist to evaluate one of your classmate's presentations.

		Good				Bad
1.	The speaker speaks clearly.	5	4	3	2	1
2.	The speaker speaks in correct sentence forms.	5	4	3	2	1
3.	The speaker gives clear reasons for his/her partner's statement.	5	4	3	2	1
4.	The speaker makes eye contact with the audience.	5	4	3	2	1

Women Still Dying in Pregnancy

Childbirth is usually a happy event that brings a new member into the family, but this is not always the case in developing countries. Many women are still dying during pregnancy and childbirth in some parts of the world. Why do they die? Are there any solutions?

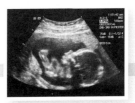

PHASE 1

1 │ Getting into the Topic

The table below shows five countries with the highest number of death in pregnancy and childbirth in 2017. Guess which countries from a–d below fit blanks 1, 3, 4, and 5.

	Country	Number of death in pregnancy and childbirth
1	( )	67,000
2	**India**	35,000
3	( )	16,000
4	( )	14,000
5	( )	11,000

Source: World Health Organization

Map of Africa

a. Tanzania	**b.** Democratic Republic of Congo	**c.** Ethiopia	**d.** Nigeria

2 | ◼◀ 1st Viewing

(online / video)

Watch the video and choose the best answers to the following questions.

1. How do the women in the video look?
   a. Comfortable
   b. Energetic
   c. Alone

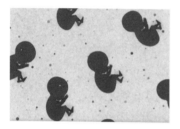

2. Where in the world do women often die during pregnancy and childbirth?
   a. In developed countries
   b. In modern countries
   c. In poor countries

PHASE 2

1 | 📋 Vocabulary

Match the words with their definitions.

1. **prevent**	☐	a.	surgery to end a pregnancy
2. **midwife**	☐	b.	a person, especially a woman, who is trained to help women give birth to babies
3. **right**	☐	c.	a moral or legal claim to have or get something or to behave in a particular way
4. **abortion**	☐	d.	the practice of treating one person or group differently from another in an unfair way
5. **discrimination**	☐	e.	to stop something from happening, or stop someone from doing something

2 📖 Reading

Read the following passage.

 DL 24 CD 24

Women in Danger – Death in Childbirth

Even though medicine has improved, about 300,000 women around the world still die each year during pregnancy or childbirth. The majority of these women live in poorer countries and war zones. However, most of these "maternal deaths" can be prevented.

5　　Many women in poor countries live far away from hospitals. It is very tiring, expensive, and dangerous for them to travel to get a checkup and to give birth. Women have to ask family members or relatives to help them give birth because there are no midwives or doctors nearby. This is very dangerous, especially when there is a problem with the pregnancy.

10　　Also, the issue of women's rights is a problem. In many poor countries, women cannot choose if and when to have children. Many women give birth to many babies in a short period of time. This is also dangerous for their health. However, they cannot prevent their pregnancies and abortion is often illegal. Thirteen percent of pregnant women's deaths are because of unsafe secret abortions. Making abortion legal would

15 actually save many women's lives around the world.

　　Death because of pregnancy is a serious problem and the United Nations (UN) wants to fix it. Leaders from countries around the world have promised to reduce the number of deaths in childbirth and pregnancy by the year 2030. However, the first step is to stop the discrimination of women. Women must be given the right to

20 control how many children they have and when. Pregnancy should be exciting and safe, not dangerous.

(253 words)

Notes

ℓ 18 **the year 2030:** The year by which the United Nations (UN) wants to reduce the number of women who die in pregnancy or childbirth. The goal is to have fewer than 70 women die per 100,000 live births by 2030.

3 | 📄 Summary

Fill in the blanks and complete the summary of the reading.

Around 300,000 women still die each year during (**p**   ) or childbirth. Most of them live in poor countries where they live far away from (**h**   ) and where (**a**   ) is illegal. World leaders want to help and the first step is to stop the (**d**   ) of women so that women have the (**r**   ) to control how many children they have and when.

PHASE 3

🔲◀ 2nd Viewing

Watch the video again and choose the best answers to the following questions.

1. About how many women who die in pregnancy or childbirth live in poor countries?

    a. 19%
    b. 99%
    c. 13%

2. Why do the women in rural areas travel many miles?

    a. To work in war zones or disaster areas
    b. To have checkups and give birth
    c. To get the right to decide if and when they have children

3. The video ends saying, "unless women can take control of their own reproduction, poorer women will continue to die needlessly." What does "reproduction" mean?

    a. Having children
    b. Discrimination
    c. Promise

PHASE 4

💬✔ **Output Task** (Writing / Speaking)

Step 1 ▶ Read the following passage and answer the questions below.

> According to the World Health Organization (WHO), the main reasons that women cannot get good healthcare during pregnancy and childbirth are: (1)they are poor, (2)they live far away from hospitals and healthcare centers, (3)they do not have information, (4)the quality of services like pre- and post-birth care is bad, and (5)their culture does not allow it.

a. Which of the above reasons do you think is the most important for reducing maternal deaths?

e.g., I think the most important problem to solve is the fact that "they are poor."

....
....

b. If you were the leader of a poor country, what would you do to solve the problem?

e.g., I would help people find jobs so that everyone can have a constant income.

....
....

Step 2 Ask a partner the questions from the previous page and complete the sentences below.

a. According to my partner _____, the most important problem
(your partner's name)

to solve is number _____, _____ .
2   "they live far away from hospitals and healthcare centers"

b. If he/she were the leader of a poor country, he/she would _____
give enough funds to local

_____ .

governments so that they could build more hospitals

Step 3 Practice the report that you made in Step 2. Then, present the report to the class.

Checklist for the Presentation

Use this checklist to evaluate one of your classmate's presentations.

Good   Bad

1. The speaker speaks clearly.   5   4   3   2   1

2. The speaker speaks in correct sentence forms.   5   4   3   2   1

3. The speaker explains his/her partner's solution to the problem.   5   4   3   2   1

4. The speaker makes eye contact with the audience.   5   4   3   2   1

UNIT 13

Struggles to Gain the Right to Vote

Have you ever heard of the city of Selma? It is a small town in Alabama in the United States with a population of about 15,000 people. It may not be familiar to those of us living in Japan, but for the people in the US, especially for African Americans, it is a place that should never be forgotten.

PHASE 1

1 | Getting into the Topic

Read the brief summary of an important US law and choose the appropriate option for each bracket.

The Voting Rights Act of 1965

— It was signed into law by President
  ¹[Lyndon B. Johnson / Martin Luther King, Jr.]
  on August 6, 1965.

— It aimed to give ²[African Americans /
  American women] their ³[freedom of speech /
  right to vote].

— Before the law, there were many
  ⁴[systems / struggles], including the incident in
  Selma.

2 ⬛◀ 1st Viewing

online/video

Watch the video and choose the best answers to the following questions.

1. According to the woman who appeared in the first scene talking to a little girl, what happened 50 years ago?
   a. A lot of people enjoyed a festival.
   b. A lot of people were killed.
   c. A lot of people painted pictures.

2. How do the black people in the video look?
   a. They look irritated.
   b. They look proud.
   c. They look sad.

PHASE 2

1 📋 Vocabulary

Match the words with their definitions.

1. **unarmed** ☐

2. **mark** ☐

3. **secure** ☐

4. **cause** ☐

5. **funding** ☐

a. an aim, belief, or movement that a group of people support or fight for

b. money given by a government or organization for an event or activity

c. not carrying any weapons

d. to celebrate an important event or occasion with a particular action

e. to get or achieve something that will be permanent, especially after a lot of effort

2 📖 Reading

Read the following passage.

Selma's Bloody Sunday
— A Day That Should Never be Forgotten

March 7, 2015 was the 50th anniversary of a civil rights march in Selma, Alabama. The peaceful march ended in violence when the police attacked unarmed protesters. The event was called Bloody Sunday because more than 50 marchers were injured. The photographs of peaceful marchers lying covered in blood in front of
5 Selma's Edmund Pettus Bridge shocked the world. After this incident, on August 6, 1965, President Lyndon B. Johnson signed the Voting Rights Act. The act significantly expanded African Americans' right to vote.

On the 50th anniversary of Bloody Sunday, many African Americans gathered in Selma to mark the occasion. This time, they were not marching to secure their right
10 to vote, but to remember the struggles their people experienced at that time. In an interview, an elderly man said that back then, he was ready to give his life to the cause. In his speech to commemorate the anniversary of Bloody Sunday, President Barack Obama said to the public: "Selma shows us that America is not the project of any one person. Because the single most powerful word in our democracy is the word, 'We.'"

15 Although a lot has changed since 1965, there are still many barriers that make it difficult for African Americans to vote. For example, there are still many black people living in poorer areas where voting stations get little funding and staffing. Many people believe that the struggle for African Americans is still not over. As one woman said, "when you forget the struggle, you repeat your past." That is why Bloody
20 Sunday should never be forgotten.   (263 words)

📎

Notes

ℓ 5 **Edmund Pettus Bridge:** a bridge across the Alabama River in Selma, known as the site of Bloody Sunday

ℓ 6 **President Lyndon B. Johnson:** the 36th president of the United States (from 1963 to 1969); an American educator and politician

ℓ 12 **President Barack Obama:** the 44th president of the United States (from 2009 to 2017); an American politician and lawyer

3  Summary

Fill in the blanks and complete the summary of the reading.

On the 50th anniversary of Bloody Sunday, in which civil rights (**p**   )
were attacked by the police, a lot of black people gathered in Selma to
(**m**   ) the occasion. Although the Voting Rights Act
(**e**   ) their right to vote, it is still difficult for poor
(**A**   ) Americans to vote. They believe that people should
never forget the (**s**   ) their people experienced at that time.

PHASE 3

■◀ 2nd Viewing

online / video

Watch the video again and choose the best answers to the following
questions.

1. What does the man showing his paintings suggest?

   a. That his paintings consist of various colors
   b. That the color of a person's skin doesn't matter
   c. That he mainly uses white, black, and yellow when painting

2. What does the woman wearing the black sunglasses say she wanted to do at the
   anniversary?

   a. She wanted to dress up to struggle.
   b. She wanted to talk to the people gathered for the anniversary.
   c. She wanted to walk the streets to feel the struggle.

3. The woman who appeared in the last scene mentions two things that black people can
   now do. One is "to vote," but what is the other?

   a. Walk down the street
   b. Wear coats
   c. Work in an office

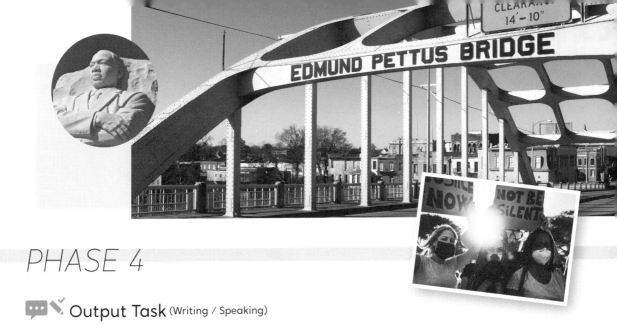

PHASE 4

💬✔ **Output Task** (Writing / Speaking)

Step 1 ▶ Do some research on civil rights activists. Choose one activist who interests you and write a brief biography about him/her. Follow the sample below.

Sample:

Martin Luther King, Jr. was **(1)**a scholar, minister, and leader of the Civil Rights Movement in the United States. He was born in **(2)**Atlanta, Georgia in 1929 and died in Memphis, Tennessee in 1968 at the age of 39. He **(3)**led the Civil Rights Movement and ended the legal segregation of African Americans in the United States. He was awarded the Nobel Peace Prize in 1964. He is also known for **(4)**his famous "I Have a Dream" speech.

_____ was/is _____.
(name)   (1) occupation

He/She was born in _____
                          (2) birth and death

_____. He/She _____
                                                        (3) best known facts/accomplishments

_____.

He/She is also know for _____
                                  (4) some other interesting information

_____.

Step 2 Share your work with a partner. Take notes about the activist that your partner researched.

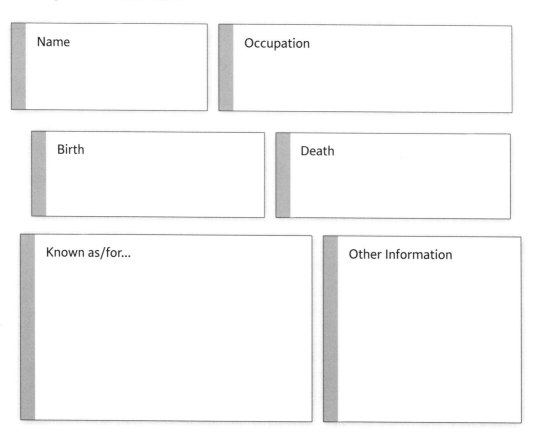

Name	Occupation

Birth	Death

Known as/for...	Other Information

Step 3 After taking notes in Step 2, ask your partner one more question and write down his/her answer to it.

Possible Questions

ⓠ *What did you like most about him/her?*

ⓠ *What can we learn from him/her?*

ⓠ *Do you know anything famous that he/she said?*

ⓠ *What would you have done if you were him/her?*

Your partner's answer

Feeling Alive Throughout Life

What will you do after you retire? Do you have any plans, such as traveling abroad or spending all day relaxing in nature? Will you be happy then? Let's take a look at the life of a 66-year-old woman who is enjoying her retirement.

PHASE 1

1 | Getting into the Topic

A British insurance company did a survey of more than 1,000 Britons over 50 years old. Guess the results and fill in the blanks with the appropriate options from a–e.

▶ **What are you looking forward to doing when you retire?**

1 ( )

2 ( )

3 ( )

4 ( )

5 ( )

a. Gardening

b. Spending more time with my friends

c. Seeing my children or grandchildren more

d. Traveling/going on holidays

e. Focusing on my existing hobbies

Source: SunLife Limited

Retirement Plan

2 | ◼◀ 1st Viewing

(online / video)

Watch the video and choose the best answers to the following questions.

1. In the video, some people are swimming in the sea.
What season do you think it is?

   a. Spring

   b. Summer

   c. Winter

2. How do the swimmers look?

   a. They look cold.

   b. They look happy.

   c. They look tired.

PHASE 2

1 | 📋 Vocabulary

Match the words with their definitions.

1. community ☐

2. retire ☐

3. workaholic ☐

4. outlook ☐

5. admit ☐

a. a group of people who have the same interests, religion, race, etc.

b. a person who chooses to work a lot and does not have time to do anything else

c. a person's point of view or general attitude to life and the world

d. to agree that something is true, especially unwillingly

e. to leave one's job and stop working, usually because the person has reached a certain age

Read the following passage.

🎧 DL 28   💿 CD 28

The Call of the Wild Sea

Wild swimming means swimming in a natural pool of water, such as the sea or a lake, instead of a man-made swimming pool. It is popular in many parts of the UK. In Plymouth, on the south coast of England, there is a community of swimmers who swim in the sea at Porthcurno Beach.

5   One member of this community is 66-year-old Julia. She started wild sea swimming when she moved to Plymouth from Italy to be with her daughter. The first winter she spent in Plymouth was cold, and Julia spent her time indoors feeling lonely. She gained 20 kg of weight. The following year, in late October, she saw a group of swimmers at Porthcurno Beach entering the cold sea. She thought, "there

10   are people swimming, and I can do it." After joining them, she fell in love with wild sea swimming and now swims with the group almost every day.

   Thinking about her life before retiring, Julia says, "I was kind of a workaholic, never having time for anything of my own." However, the exercise from wild sea swimming changed not only her body, but her outlook. "It's freedom. It's joy. It's

15   pleasure. It's a birthday party," she says. For her, swimming is going back to being a child and getting away from her problems and thoughts. She admits that there are some days that she does not feel like swimming, but says that what pushes her is the people around her. "You think, the others are going to be out there waiting for me, I've got to go," she says with a smile.   (271 words)

Porthcurno Beach

Notes

ℓ 3   **Plymouth:** A port town in southwestern England. It is famous for being where the Pilgrims boarded their ship, the Mayflower, and set out for the New World (now the United States of America) in the year 1620.

ℓ 4   **Porthcurno:** a small seaside village on the southwestern coast of England, located near the resort town of Penzance where the swimming scene was shot

3 📄 Summary

DL 29　　⦿ CD 29

Fill in the blanks and complete the summary of the reading.

Julia, a 66-year-old woman, is now a member of a wild sea swimming group. After (r　　　　　　　), she moved from Italy to Plymouth, but she was feeling lonely. One day, she saw some people at Porthcurno Beach (s　　　　　　　) in the cold sea. She joined them and now enjoys swimming almost every day. She says that the exercise from wild sea swimming changed not only her body, but her (o　　　　　　　). Although she (a　　　　　　　) that she sometimes does not feel like swimming, she goes there because she knows other members will be (w　　　　　　) for her.

PHASE 3

🎥 2nd Viewing

Watch the video again and choose the best answers to the following questions.

1. About how long did Julia stay in the water when she first entered the sea?

　a. About 20 seconds
　b. About 30 seconds
　c. About 40 seconds

2. What kind of post-retirement plan did Julia have?

　a. She planned to enjoy wild swimming.
　b. She planned to do some physical exercise.
　c. She had no plan.

3. Julia says, "You have to push yourself to some limits." What does she mean?

　a. You have to make a great effort.
　b. You have to know your own limitations.
　c. You have to limit your actions.

PHASE 4

💬✓ Output Task (Writing / Speaking)

Step I ▶ Think about your life after retirement in the future. Answer the questions below.

a. What kind of post-retirement life do you want to have?

e.g., I want to enjoy climbing mountains, such as Mt. Iwaki and Mt. Tateyama.

b. What are your concerns about your post-retirement life?

e.g., I'm worried about my health.

c. What are you going to do to achieve your ideal life in the future?

e.g., I'm going to continue doing physical exercise regularly.

Step 2 Put your answers from Step 1 a–c into a report on your post-retirement plan.

e.g., I want to enjoy climbing mountains in Japan, but I'm worried about my health. For this reason, I am going to continue doing physical exercise regularly.

Step 3 Share your plans with your classmates and write down their answers.

Name	Post-retirement Life	Concerns	What to Do
Cathy	climbing mountains	health	regular exercise
Takeru	traveling the world	money	monthly savings

📋 Vocabulary List

This is a list of useful words/phrases that can help you to better understand the videos/readings in this textbook. You may use it to prepare for class, review, or however you choose.

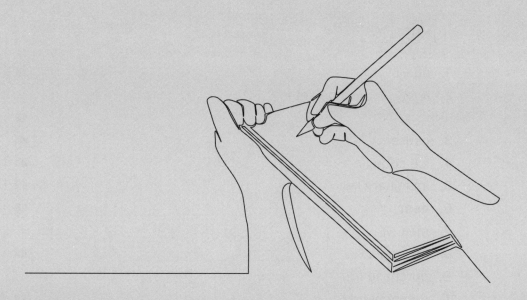

Vocabulary List

Write down the meaning of each word/phrase below.

from the video / from the reading

[n] = noun / [v] verb / [adj] adjective / [adv] adverb

UNIT 1

1. clue [n]
2. comfort [n]
3. definitely [adv]
4. degree [n]
5. entire [adj]
6. equipment [n]
7. latest [adj]
8. luxury [adj]
9. pillow [n]
10. provide [v]
11. put on [v]
12. thick [adj]
13. unusual [adj]
14. yell [v]

UNIT 2

1. ad [n]
2. (a novel, film, etc.) be set in

3. cause [v]
4. ice cube [n]
5. imaginary [adj]
6. item [n]
7. melt [v]
8. no longer
9. purchase [n]
10. recommend [v]
11. remind [v]

12. survival kit [n]

13. take shelter

14. temperature [n]

15. water level [n]

UNIT 3

1. add [v]

2. bare [adj]

3. be [get] used to

4. celebration [n]

5. chew [v]

6. chunk [n]

7. for the first time

8. hold [v]

9. odd [adj]

10. raw [adj]

11. slice [v]

12. thin [adj]

13. wipe [v]

14. yellowtail [n]

UNIT 4

1. annoy [v]

2. behavior [n]

3. bully [v]

4. diabetes [n]

5. feather [n]

6. feed [v]

7. garbage [n]

8. generally [adv]

9. hate [v]

10. lid [n]

11. mess [n]

12. nuisance [n]

13. pick at

14. rip off

15. screech [v]

16. scream [v]

UNIT 5

1. accuracy [n]

2. article [n]

3. curious [adj]

4. describe [v]

5. employ [v]

6. fairly [adv]

7. lie [v]

8. matter [v]

9. organize [v]

10. politician [n]

11. powerless [adj]

12. pride oneself on

13. properly [adv]

14. prove [v]

15. publish [v]

16. responsible [adj]

17. subscriber [n]

UNIT 6

1. absurd [adj]

2. bill [n]

3. colleague [n]

4. combine [v]

5. fix [v]

6. hassle [n]

7. improvement [n]

8. income [n]

9. nightmare [n]

10. occur [v]

11. pause [v]

12. payment [n] _____
13. poverty [n] _____
14. pretence [n] _____
15. reform [n] _____
16. rent [n] _____
17. rollout [n] _____
18. starve [v] _____
19. take out loans _____
20. transition [n] _____

UNIT 7

1. aviation [n] _____
2. coal [n] _____
3. currently [adv] _____
4. deliver [v] _____
5. electricity [n] _____
6. essential [adj] _____
7. feed [v] _____
8. generate [v] _____
9. household [n] _____
10. invention [n] _____
11. overtake [v] _____
12. pollute [v] _____
13. potentially [adv] _____
14. renewable [adj] _____
15. rural [adj] _____
16. supply [n] _____
17. source [n] _____
18. waste [v] _____

UNIT 8

1. actually [adv] _____
2. app [n] _____
3. attitude [n] _____
4. charity [n] _____

5. earn [v]

6. expert [n]

7. explode [v]

8. generation [n]

9. massive [adj]

10. resale [n]

11. spring up

12. stack up

13. stuff [n]

14. sustainability [n]

15. tool [n]

16. up to

17. variety [n]

18. wardrobe [n]

UNIT 9

1. allow [v]

2. authorization [n]

3. a variety of

4. display [v]

5. figurine [n]

6. fix [v]

7. object [n]

8. public [n]

9. retire [v]

10. sanitation [n]

11. store [v]

12. trash [n]

13. throw away

14. whole [adj]

UNIT 10

1. activist [n]

2. arrest [n, v]

3. attempt [n]

4. catastrophe [n]
5. crisis [n]
6. emergency [n]
7. face [v]
8. imprisonment [n]
9. inspire [v]
10. intentionally [adv]
11. optimistic [adj]
12. policy [n]
13. provoke [v]
14. refuse [v]
15. sacrifice [n]

UNIT 11

1. architecture [n]
2. belonging [n]
3. browse [v]
4. bulk [n]
5. experiment [n]
6. material [n]
7. minimum [n]
8. neighborhood [n]
9. profile [n]
10. relationship [n]
11. slightly [adv]
12. stock [v]

UNIT 12

1. checkup [n]
2. childbirth [n]
3. disaster [n]
4. give birth (to)
5. go wrong
6. improve [v]
7. issue [n]

8. legal [adj]

9. maternal [adj]

10. medicine [n]

11. pregnancy [n]

12. reduce [v]

13. relative [n]

14. tiring [adj]

15. war zone [n]

UNIT 13

1. Act [n]

2. civil rights [n]

3. commemorate [v]

4. democracy [n]

5. gather [v]

6. incident [n]

7. injured [adj]

8. march [n]

9. occasion [n]

10. vote [v]

11. voting station

UNIT 14

1. euphoria [n]

2. fall in love with

3. following [adj]

4. gain (...kg, weight, etc.)

5. get away from

6. have got to do

7. hibernate [v]

8. man-made [adj]

9. occurrence [n]

10. pleasure [n]

Video Credit

All the videos in *INTEGRITY* are originally taken from *the Guardian*.

Unit 1 The Thai tourist hotel that is a prison: inside Bangkok's latest place to stay (September 01, 2017)
www.theguardian.com/world/video/2017/sep/01/the-thai-tourist-hotel-that-is-a-prison-inside-bangkoks-latest-place-to-stay-video

Unit 2 Climate change bargains: the hottest deals of 2056 (July 17, 2015)
www.theguardian.com/environment/video/2015/jul/17/climate-change-deals-future-ucb-comedy-video

Unit 3 How to make sushi with friends (August 10, 2013)
www.theguardian.com/lifeandstyle/video/2013/aug/10/how-to-make-your-own-sushi-video

Unit 4 On the trail of Australia's naughtiest cockatoo (November 03, 2019)
www.theguardian.com/global/video/2019/nov/03/on-the-trail-of-australias-naughtiest-cockatoo-video

Unit 5 Changing the world for the better': Katharine Viner tells us about her role (November 28, 2018)
www.theguardian.com/newswise/video/2018/nov/28/changing-the-world-for-the-better-katharine-viner-tells-us-about-her-role-video

Unit 6 Absurd and degrading: how universal credit can ruin lives (October 24, 2018)
www.theguardian.com/society/video/2018/oct/24/absurd-and-degrading-how-universal-credit-ruins-lives-video

Unit 7 How keeping cool is making us hot (October 26, 2015)
www.theguardian.com/environment/video/2015/oct/26/keeping-cool-making-us-hot-video-animation-climate-change

Unit 8 How the resale revolution is reshaping fashion (February 20, 2020)
www.theguardian.com/global/video/2020/feb/20/how-the-resale-revolution-is-reshaping-fashion-video-explainer

Unit 9 Treasures in the trash: the amazing things New Yorkers throw away (December 22, 2014)
www.theguardian.com/us-news/video/2014/dec/22/new-york-trash-museum-video

Unit 10 The climate protesters ready to go to prison for the planet (November 14, 2018)
www.theguardian.com/environment/video/2018/nov/14/the-climate-protesters-ready-to-go-to-prison-for-the-planet-video

Unit 11 The New Yorkers who live exclusively via Airbnb (June 14, 2016)
www.theguardian.com/cities/video/2016/jun/14/new-yorkers-who-live-exclusively-via-airbnb-video

Unit 12 Why do women still die in childbirth, asks Emily Watson (May 16, 2016)
www.theguardian.com/global-development/video/2016/may/16/why-do-women-still-die-in-childbirth-asks-emily-watson-video

Unit 13 Bloody Sunday veterans in Selma, Alabama, 50 years on (March 09, 2015)
www.theguardian.com/us-news/video/2015/mar/09/bloody-sunday-veterans-selma-alabama-video?CMP=gu_com

Unit 14 Wild sea swimming in my 60s: 'it erases problems, it's being a child again' (February 13, 2017)
www.theguardian.com/society/video/2017/feb/13/wild-sea-swimming-in-my-60s-erases-problems-being-child-again-video

Photo Credit

(p.5) © Ahmad Faizal Yahya | Dreamstime.com

(p.9) TM & © TOHO CO., LTD. (Phase 1.1 Getting into the Topic [left])

(p.27) © Barbara Klump / Max Planck Institute of Animal Behavior (Phase 1.1 Getting into the Topic)

(p.63) © Laurence Agron | Dreamstime.com (Phase 1.1 Getting into the Topic [top])
© Simone Hogan | Dreamstime.com (Phase 1.1 Getting into the Topic [middle])
© Antonello Marangi | Dreamstime.com (Phase 1.1 Getting into the Topic [bottom])

(p.81) © LBJ Library photo by Yoichi Okamoto (Phase 1.1 Getting into the Topic)

(p.89) © Simon Gurney | Dreamstime.com

このテキストのメインページ
www.kinsei-do.co.jp/plusmedia/41
次のページの QR コードを読み取る
直接ページにジャンプできます

オンライン映像配信サービス「plus⁺Media」について

本テキストの映像は plus⁺Media ページ（www.kinsei-do.co.jp/plusmedia）から、ストリーミング再生でご利用いただけます。手順は以下に従ってください。

ログイン

- ●ご利用には、ログインが必要です。
  サイトのログインページ（www.kinsei-do.co.jp/plusmedia/login）へ行き、plus⁺Media パスワード（次のページのシールをはがしたあとに印字されている数字とアルファベット）を入力します。

- ●パスワードは各テキストにつき1つです。
  有効期限は、<u>はじめてログインした時点から1年間</u>になります。

ログインページ

[利用方法]

次のページにある QR コード、もしくは plus⁺Media トップページ（www.kinsei-do.co.jp/plusmedia）から該当するテキストを選んで、そのテキストのメインページにジャンプしてください。

plus+Media トップ　　　　メインページ

メニューページ　　　　再生画面

「Video」「Audio」をタッチすると、それぞれのメニューページにジャンプしますので、そこから該当する項目を選べば、ストリーミングが開始されます。

[推奨環境]

iOS (iPhone, iPad)	OS: iOS 12 以降 ブラウザ：標準ブラウザ	Android	OS: Android 6 以降 ブラウザ：標準ブラウザ、Chrome
PC	OS: Windows 7/8/8.1/10, MacOS X　ブラウザ：Internet Explorer 10/11, Microsoft Edge, Firefox 48以降, Chrome 53以降, Safari		

※最新の推奨環境についてはウェブサイトをご確認ください。
※上記の推奨環境を満たしている場合でも、機種によってはご利用いただけない場合もあります。また、推奨環境は技術動向等により変更される場合があります。予めご了承ください。

このシールをはがすと plus+Media 利用のためのパスワードが記載されています。

一度はがすと元に戻すことはできませんのでご注意下さい。

◀ ここからはがして下さい

4174 INTEGRITY Beginner plus+Media

本書にはCD（別売）があります

INTEGRITY　Beginner

Vitalize Your English Studies with Authentic Videos

海外メディア映像から深める　4技能・教養英語【初級編】

2023年1月20日　初版第1刷発行
2023年2月20日　初版第2刷発行

編著者	竹 内　　理
	佐々木　顕　彦
	川　光　大　介
	森　安　瑞　希
発行者	福　岡　正　人
発行所　株式会社	金 星 堂

（〒101-0051）　東京都千代田区神田神保町 3-21
Tel　（03）3263-3828（営業部）
　　　（03）3263-3997（編集部）
Fax　（03）3263-0716
https://www.kinsei-do.co.jp

編集担当　蔦原美智・長島吉成　　　　　　　　Printed in Japan
印刷所・製本所／萩原印刷株式会社

ISBN978-4-7647-4174-4　C1082